A Mystic Garden

Also by Gunilla Norris

Being Home

Becoming Bread

Journeying in Place

Inviting Silence

A
Mystic
Garden

Working with Soil, Attending to Soul

Gunilla Norris

BlueBridge

Jacket design by Amy C. King
Jacket photography by Corbis
Text design by Jennifer Ann Daddio
Illustrations by John Giuliani

Library of Congress Cataloging-in-Publication Data
Norris, Gunilla Brodde, 1939-
A mystic garden : working with soil,
attending to soul/Gunilla Norris.
p. cm.
ISBN 1-933346-01-9
1. Gardens—Religious aspects—Meditations.
2. Seasons—Religious aspects—Meditations.
3. Norris, Gunilla Brodde, 1939–. I. Title.
BL624.2.N68 2006
204'.35—dc22
2005035490

Published by
BLUEBRIDGE
An imprint of United Tribes Media Inc.
240 West 35th Street, Suite 500
New York, NY 10001

www.bluebridgebooks.com

Printed in the United States of America

10 9 8 7 6 5 4 3 2 1

Contents

FOR STANLEY,

my beloved partner,

AND THE GARDEN WE SHARE

In the garden more grows
than the gardener sows.

SPANISH PROVERB

A Mystic Garden

Introduction

To have a garden, even a small one, is a great privilege. Working with soil, with seeds and plants I find I must live a different kind of time. Growth, both inner and outer, has its own rhythm, and if I am to really be present I must be with organic time, with seasonal changes, with weather and waiting, with hard work and trust, and with disappointment and surrender. I know in the end that while I garden I am the one who will be cultivated. It will be my inner soil that will be worked. I will be the one pruned and weeded. If there is any integration, peace, and fruitfulness, it will come by grace.

Stanley and I live in a neighborhood that once was a large New England farm. Our yellow house has a Japanese maple tree in front. Most of the garden is in the back. There is a schoolyard nearby, and most days we can hear the children's laughter at recess. A line of juniper trees marks the north border of our property and makes a haven for birds and squirrels. In the soft soil under one of our rhododendron bushes, a rabbit has its burrow. Despite the neighborhood cats that love to hunt here, this little rabbit helps himself to the lettuce in the beds of vegetables behind the garage. Stanley and I share the garden with friends and family and with creatures that call this place home as much as we do, even though they don't pay the taxes. It is a communal garden.

One day in the future this place will be sold and I will move on, or I will be carried away and the garden will continue in whatever manner it does. Why then this inexplicable love of poking in the earth, getting sunburned, stung by nettles, bitten by ants, and finding, after many months, only one tomato on the vine? It's hard to explain unless you find yourself up to your elbows in the process. This is equally true for the work of contemplation.

A garden tends to get inside us. If we go there to accomplish something or get something, the garden soon becomes a burden. With expectations that it must look good or that it has to produce no matter what, we will soon grow tired. The garden is really a place in which we can give ourselves away. This is true of any serious contemplation, too. We are transformed by it. We are reduced and revealed by it. In it we may experience a lived sense of our connection to the earth, to our inner freedom, and to the Sacred, the ground of our existence.

For me gardening is a process that invites me to be fully engaged. It is also a constant exercise in letting go since so much happens that is not in my control. Strangely this duality seems to cultivate a joy that embraces impermanence and finds refuge in the invisible.

Gardening brings food and flowers to the table and sustenance to the soul. I am not talking of having a perfect garden. Ours certainly isn't! Weeds are as happy here as are flowers. Bushes get bushier and need trimming. What may start out as an elegant garden plan becomes more haphazard over time. With the years our garden has turned out to be a bit of this and that and always too big to really tend properly.

From the start this is not the garden I designed. Someone else did, and before that there was a yard of sorts. Coming here to live I have inherited what already was, just as I inherited my parents, my siblings, and my particular time in history. We work with what we are given. That's the real garden. I can't claim anything here. I can only "be" in the garden, tend it, and further it. Isn't that what we all do, what life asks us to do?

Working in my garden I find it a place that mirrors for me the dark and the light of my mind. After all, whatever I project on my garden is not the real garden. I know that! But it is the garden I perceive with whatever level of awareness I have, and it is the only garden I can work in. Hence, the book's subtitle. In my garden while I am digging I am also tilling inner soil. My garden is a place of commitment and neglect, of arrogance and humility. It is a place of taking stock and of deep silence—a place of contemplation. And so for me over time it has become a place of grace.

I experience as the particular human being I am. I have no choice about that, but I trust that I am more like other people than not, and that what I find working the soil might also be what others find working theirs. I want to trust that with reverence for place and awareness of my foibles, I can grow to be more present and a better steward of my small corner of the earth.

This book is about a whole year in a garden. I invite you to read it slowly, just as I wrote it slowly. During that process, phrases and thoughts sprung to mind—not in long sentences but in thought bursts. And I found that another voice wanted to speak as well. What voice was that?

I sensed I was in dialogue with something earthy that was old and wise. Perhaps it was the soil itself. It felt like a grounding voice, a sage of sorts. So I wrote down what

I imagined it to be saying. It had another point of view and acted like an antidote or addition to what I was thinking and feeling.

The great physicist Niels Bohr said, "There are two types of truth. In the shallow type, the opposite of a true statement is false. In the deeper kind, the opposite of a true statement is equally true." I hope you will add your true statements, your insights, your disagreements, and your epiphanies. Then we might grow something together and tend both the soil in our flowerbeds and the soil within.

Gunilla Norris
Mystic, Connecticut

Winter

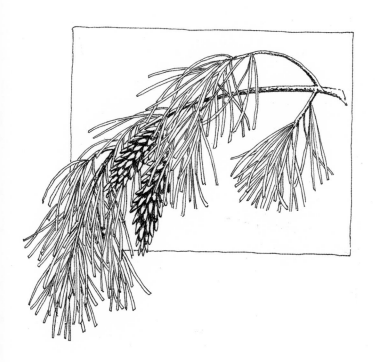

Winter

The solstice is marked in our calendars. It is the traditional date for the beginning of winter. We like to trust our calendars because they allow us to agree where to meet and when to do certain things. They give us some sense of control over our destinies. We divide time and structure it to suit us, fitting our lives into neat little squares—a whole year kept safe between covers. Calendars help us keep track of ourselves and allow us to feel an illusion of safety.

But when time is marked differently, when it is a way of attending to the moment, we will *experience* the beginning of winter. For me it is the first day the temperature slips below thirty-two. It is the day the nasturtiums turn into a soggy mess, when the impatiens sag into a heap. Winter begins with a deathblow. Something is absolutely clear—we are not in charge. The trees are stripped. Only the evergreens are left with their blue-green darkness.

Now is the time for no thing. We are invited to enter this mystery. Frost is the teacher that shows us we would not survive a day without a home and heat. And our souls, too, know something our outer selves do not register most of the time: in winter we have the chance to enter a clear, empty space. Whenever something ends, something else has begun. Our souls can dive into the biting cold, into darkness, into bare being. The unknown is there. There is no calendar, no time. No self-definition. Winter is a womb in which to grow.

The wind blows. The cold deepens. Something within us quickens and stirs.

The First of November

In old agrarian calendars the first of November, All Saint's Day, was the beginning of the new year. Today is gray and cold. The air is charged with the coming frost.

Could we take that leap of faith that now is when gardening begins, with an approaching end? Soon the ground will be frozen solid, the grass covered with early snow. Everything will grow quiet in the cold's embrace.

What is wrong with feeling joy in this clout of cold? When something is over, it's over—no doubt, no turning back, no illusion. Winter's big hit is a kind of liberation. It's a chance to stop, to turn our backs on effort. We can let ourselves rest. We can turn within.

This is true for great losses in life. A clean acceptance of them is finally freedom. The slow recovery from grief is a winter season of sleep, of rest and allowing things to be. It is trusting, rather, that "what is" just now will move us to "what can be." Joy and loss are together. Loss cauterizes, and grief, when fully accepted, opens us to new life, to a mysterious, inexplicable joy.

Any love that has been experienced
is not lost.
It returns to Love itself.

How full of invisible life
is the garden you've been given.

At this very moment,
you are in company with everything.
Trust does not need visible signs.

Sleet

The weather growls, hisses, screams against the window. Trees are coated with ice. The bushes sag with the weight. Car doors freeze shut.

Out there, the garden lies mute under this howling. Silently it shows how to be in the presence of storm.

"Accept. Be still. Stay inside. Stay inside."

The trees will be diamonds
when the sun comes out.

Ice and Beauty,
Howling Wind.
These are also the names of God!

Dying Daily

The garden is under three feet of snow. In some places I can't even see the trimmed roses poking up out of the drifts. The taller raspberry canes and hydrangeas are like a man's two-day stubble on a white chin.

Now the tarragon has gone underground. Near the house corner where it is warm, the clematis vine is a crumble of brown leaves and stems. It looks like a heap of tea leaves someone spilled in great haste.

Everything is dormant in the cold. My spirit, too, is spilled and scattered. I seem to be at a standstill. Do I know that? Or is it that, connected to God, one somehow moves forward even in sleep, in confusion, in turmoil, in cold? Benumbed, we may wonder if perhaps it is in quietude, in seeming deep freeze, that God enters our depth without interference?

Below the ever-tracking mind, can we sense, trust, or feel the soul being led? Could we learn to simply accept this, to allow it?

Our ego's self-importance is always there, and so is our wavering. How impossible it often seems to give ourselves over, to accept the cauterizing cold, the surrender of well-laid plans, the necessity to die daily to live.

Continuing to ask questions
is a way for the mind to make itself important,
to pretend it has control.

Let go.
You are *dying daily.*

Doing Nothing

It's too early for anything to be done in the garden. The sun pours down—a promise of the warming to come. In a day or two, however, the temperature will drop below freezing again. I can be fairly sure of that. Now is a time of waiting.

I sit down on the makeshift bench against the back of the garage. The vegetable beds lie before me. I lean back.

What do we do when we wait? Plan? Fidget? Fret? Dream? Rest? Pace? Why is it so hard to do nothing? The simplest, easiest thing is to let things be. Why not just "be" in the sun this little moment? Perhaps when we do nothing we see how naked we feel without plans? Perhaps we feel useless without our goals? To be without agenda—is that not the most lovingly present and accepting anyone can be?

The earth is ancient and spacious—
a millennial presence with no hurry,
no anxiety.

You've emerged from that patience.
It took countless years for your kind
to evolve, to stand on firm ground.

What is one of your months with such a perspective?

January Thaw

It's balmy out, a winter tease. I take off my jacket, walk in the garden where everything is wet, soaked through. I leave footprints, the rubber treads of someone in a sleep-walking dream who somehow woke up in sunshine.

Can a warming thaw penetrate to the coldest parts of us? Why is it so hard to be undefended, to allow ourselves to be like the ground, opened and moistened?

Why question gifts?

Embrace warmth
when you feel it,
allow earth to support you
when you stand on it.

Mud Season

The grass is intensely green next to patches of lingering snow. This is the time between—neither winter, nor spring. So much is invisible now, yet deep down there is a burgeoning, an unstoppable force.

The ground is saturated. Life teems below the surface. Right now, in this messy, volatile weather—one day warm, the next day freezing—a transition is happening. Can we trust our own confused, inner mud season as much as the one outside the window? Can we trust that what is not now visible in our lives will emerge one day?

Somewhere in the Talmud it is said that every blade of grass has its own angel whispering, "Grow. Grow!" Are we too sophisticated for angels, too proud to be helped? What would happen if we listened for that loving whisper meant for us?

There is a common saying—
"If something can go wrong,
it will."

But the opposite is truer.
"If something can go right,
it will,
it must!"

Spring

Spring

The plants have been resting out of sight and deep within winter. They've been gathering potential for the next season. Some have died when the weather and their general health conspired to end their lifespan. Perhaps more goes on in the winter of the soul than any of us can imagine. No wonder we feel elated when we see the first shy green shoots of a snowdrop. "Now here, here is the beginning," we might think. This is not true, of course. The beginning was long before these signs.

What we see is rather a continuance. And in the inner life there may be a danger that we give new little shoots too much attention and significance. When something is greening inside us, might it not be best to shelter the tender growth? Too much windy talk about what is going on or too much conscious sunlight can blast or kill the development of what is young and emerging. We must foster rather than force.

Spring is an ache. Buds swell on their branches. Bulbs cannot stay in their casings. There is the breaking out of one state into another. This is true in inner development as well. We are both the ones giving birth and the birthed. We are incredibly vulnerable, beautiful, dependent, dynamic, needy, and bursting at the seams.

The Spring of the soul hums and aches. Birthing is full of pain, full of fear, full of exquisite excitement. It must be carefully attended. It must also be left well enough alone. Whatever has the dynamism to develop cannot be stopped. It will grow. It will grow.

Looking Things Over

It's too early in the season to do much but look things over, to walk around and survey the winter's damage and the hopeful signs of spring.

The ground is soggy. Old leaves pack in among the bushes looking barren now without their leaves. How like this are the seasonal moods of the soul—now muddy, now bright, now soggy, needing the warming light of God's presence! All we can do is notice, gaze, and see the bare truth of our situation.

I stand in my inner garden and in the actual garden. There is so much work to do, but I know the time for action is not yet. My arms hang by my sides. The tools are in the basket. I try hard to believe the old saying, "They also serve who only stand and wait."

The air feels metallic. It's time to go inside again, into more waiting.

With or without your hard work
God is always moving
in your life.

Wait on the Holy,
wait and receive the gifts that come.

Light

Daylight comes earlier now that it's spring. Birds sing even in the dark. Dormant life stirs in the garden. Inside, I am stirring, too, waking up from something sleepy and inert, something that's held me quiet in the cold.

After a long winter we may feel a new permission. Isn't this when the gardening begins to begin? It's time to raise the blinds and open the windows as well, to let air in, even if it's cold. It's time for new life to touch our faces and our inward being.

The light is there. We can ask now to really be wakened.

The dark has its own ray.
It is part of day.

To be illumined
by not knowing, not seeing,
not doing is also a way.

Even in the deepest darkness
are you not still with God?

Limiting the Scope

In deciding to grow anything, don't I need to describe the space it needs? Don't I need to limit the scope of what I am attempting?

How often I have taken on too much or found I have failed in trust and made my intention too small! How big is the border, the vegetable bed, the raspberry patch, our work in the world, our capacity to maintain and sustain what we start? Will we let ourselves make proper limits— to do just what we can do—and no more?

What we put on our plates can bloat us or starve us. That is true of food and activity. Today, what is a just limit, a joyous limit, a comfortable limit? Can we be helped to know what is enough and to live it?

Balance is in the very order of things.
Mistakes correct themselves,
sometimes very harshly.

In time overwork will make you sick.
You will be forced to stop.
Doing nothing, you will wither
into nothing.

God's loving patience is endless.
It is only a matter of time
before the mighty are fallen and
the humble are raised up.

Dressing for the Job

The oldest pair of jeans, sweatshirt with paint spills, the parka with a split seam in the sleeve and those big pockets, last year's sneakers, soft cotton scarf, muddy gloves, and I'm dressed for the job in comfort clothes—ones I can ignore and feel free in, ones that give me room to reach, to crouch, to sit on bare ground.

I lose a sense of myself in these clothes. They are more like a second skin. Now the garden is the focus. I am free to be in it and with it.

Is this not the way of prayer as well—to be so self-forgetting as to lose ourselves in God's presence?

Consider the lilies of the field.
There is no raiment like theirs.

The beauty and use God gives
to every part of the creation
is always there
if you are willing to see it.

Your raiment has already been given.
It fits you perfectly.

Spring Cleaning

The birds are up at four in the morning. It seems they don't want to waste a single moment or delay the need and the pleasure of singing their mating songs.

Something ancient wakes in spring. It asks, "Where have you been? Where do you think life takes place, in slumber? Pull the dead chard stumps, the decaying cabbage roots—pull them like old teeth from the ground."

Spring cleaning is a time to release what we are hiding. The room such things take robs us of new life. Now is the time to gather the old from under those sneaky bushes where things tend to hide. Now is the time to throw the worn into the compost pile. Now is the time to turn the soil, to be open to renewal. Now is the time to ask for new leaves.

They who clean too much leave no cover.
Spare a little shelter for the young.

They who clean too fast have no trust.
The past will pass in its own good
and inevitable time.

Old Friends

Snowdrops, the daring ones are first. Their white bells hang in the sunlight and the cold. I am so glad to see them.

Then soon after, the crocuses give me their thumbs-up. Primroses open their bright faces! It is as if old friends have come back to visit again after a long absence. It seems easy to resume where we left off.

This is true for loved people. We share another season, celebrate that life goes on, that we are still together. But the stunning moments are there, too, when a dear one dies. The inexorable truth comes home—every moment lived is also a moment gone.

I see the winterkill now. Why must I be brought to feel gratefulness through loss? To love, to grow this garden, to appreciate the spring is fullness and ache. We always live in paradox.

Nostalgia is sweet
and full of poison.

Why think it so important
to go on,
and to keep going on?

Why cling to thinking
of the future and the past?

The present is forever.
There is never anything else.

Digging

What happens when I dig? The earth breaks. The invisible is made visible—stones, roots, sand, clay. I can see what is there and the rocks that need removing, the humus to add.

I step up on the blade and hold the handle. My whole body's weight is needed to push through the surface. I have to do it many times before I can lift what I've loosened and turn it over. Digging is hard work I've never grown used to.

This is true for inner digging, too. Yet, from time to time we simply must do it to know what's under a feeling, a dream, an unwarranted action, a persistent mood. Under the surface is soil that must be spaded up to be able to see the truth. It's mostly unpleasant.

Acknowledging our stubborn, hidden layers is humbling. Long-held attitudes of isolation, self-pity, resentment, regret, and despair come to the surface. They lie scattered like heavy stones all around us. We are broken. We are clay. Rabbi Menachem Mendel of Kotzk once said, "Nothing is more whole than a broken heart." Our hearts are broken many times throughout life. If only we could feel then that we are whole!

Breathed by God
clay begins to live.

See how there is no part of creation
that is found unworthy of being.

Drainage

Now that the bed has been dug down a foot or more below the boards, there is room for a layer of gravel—loose stones for water to drain through. This layer is important. With too much standing water there will be root rot. Drainage is one way the garden breathes.

How does a life breathe? Do we pack too much into our circumstances and have no room for runoff? Not everything in life can be absorbed into awareness. Deep down we need loose shale through which many things can pass: grief we cannot fully accept, frustrations that are not appropriate to express.

We need drainage instead of the bedrock that forces pain to stay and accumulate. We need willingness to let things pass through, and trust that there is enough ease and grace for us to let things filter out and be held in the love of God. Slowly we can find the wisdom that allows everything to pass but the essential.

No matter how much
you think,
prepare,
try,
and otherwise arrange
the circumstances of your life,
there will always be circumstances.

What can be let go of,
leaves in God's time,
even without your willing it.

Making the Bed

Here it is then, three feet by five feet—a place for greens, a box of hope. It has plenty of sunlight but it's also closer to the garage, and therefore shade lasts longer into the day. That is good for lettuce.

The sides of the bed are almost a foot tall. This is a space with a specific purpose. I am not confused about what should be here—good soil and a variety of lettuces.

In the house I have a space just for prayer and contemplation. It's a space to help me stay on purpose, to not be confused about what I am doing. Even so, all kinds of things crowd into my mind and heart. Thinking, planning, drifting, it's hard to leave room for just being in the presence of God. I'm boxed in by old habits.

Limitations are necessary for development and growth. Any limitation can be a prison or a place of freedom. It depends on our attitudes. I need to accept that I can't grow cabbage and broccoli and tomatoes all in the same place. I have to keep to one or two crops to grow anything decent here. This kind of limitation is true about a lot of things. In contemplation especially, the willingness to be confined to deep listening, to patient stability, is a proven way to root into God. This can feel like a kind of pregnancy if we will only stay quiet, if we don't interrupt what is really happening. No wonder it was said of pregnant women that they were "confined" with child.

"The way you make your bed
is the way you will lie in it,"
says the proverb.

And even perfectly made,
"the best-laid plans go oft awry."

There is no way except the very one
you are on.
Confine yourself to that
and find that you are pregnant with life,
that new things are constantly born.

Soil

Sphagnum moss, compost, sand, ordinary garden soil, a little lime, perhaps, or maybe nothing—all of it needs to be turned with a fork. I turn, lift, lighten, dig, and mix.

I want the bed to be rich and mounded. I want the soil to fill the box to the brim, to bursting. We want so much all the time while our inner ground lies inert and helpless. Being so busy, busy, busy, we are completely taken up with our urgent wants. No fork can turn the inner soil.

Deep within it is dark. As I work in this lettuce box I feel an ache, a longing to be turned, to be set right. Oh, that the work of our hands and the meditations of our hearts could always be one!

What you gaze on, gazes back.

What you contemplate in faithfulness,
changes you into itself.

Turning and turning you'll come around
to being
open like earth
in which much can grow.

First Planting

Here is the moment for which I have been waiting so many months. The packet is open. The seeds lie inside full of promise, dry and potent. Some are so small they can hardly be handled. This is the season for arugula and lettuce—the daring early crop that can tolerate wet, cool weather.

I make shallow furrows, sprinkle in the seeds. Then they are tamped down with a thin layer of earth. Here's the lettuce bed, full of intention and hope.

Can we remember that every thought we have is seed also and that we plant seeds inside ourselves all the time? Our inner gardens have thistles and ragweed as well as marigolds and sunflowers.

Our thoughts may seem small to us, almost insignificant, not unlike the lettuce seeds put in the ground. But they can grow into significance. Our lives develop from them and in many ways they determine our existence.

How can we realize what we plant daily? How do we bare this responsibility?

Seeds germinate in the dark,
sink their roots, develop stems.
It is the way of thought also.

Only when what has been invisible
breaks the surface can you see
what to weed,
what to feed and water.

Roses

The roses lie on the burlap sack in the sturdy cardboard box they came packed in. Their roots are bare. On a printed sheet the planting instructions are next to them. How vulnerable they are in transit. Without quick transportation in that sturdy container, a good reception, and a quick placement in the garden, they are done for.

We are so much like them, sliding into the world with the root to our mother exposed. We must be received to grow in this world. We must be swaddled, sheltered, and fed. Even as adults we need this. How vulnerable life is without support. If we have no place, we are rootless. It is hard to become "that part of God" we were born for without being planted securely in life.

My spiritual core will be a thorny twig with shriveled roots if I am not planted in God's presence. Along with these roses I need to be placed in deep soil, in quiet loam, in the tenderness of God.

We need living water for our thirst. We need to be fed and tended by the generous life force that is at the heart of all things. Only then can our potential come to greening. The greatest longing is to leaf out, to become what we have been given to be.

How strange and mysterious
are the ways of God.

Not *greening,* not *flowering*
may be a path
to the center as well.

Acceptance of yourself
as you are
and others as they are
is the true potting soil.
All growth starts there.

Summer

Summer

The warmth has come. Now, in mid-June, I can go into the garden with bare feet and shoulders. Stripped down, I can live without the usual layers. I see how thirsty the ground is, even this early in the season. I realize how thirsty I am—deeply, inwardly thirsty. All around me I feel powerful urges. Urges to grow and develop hum in the air. Is that what we mean by urgency? The ground shouts for water. Leaves turn eagerly towards the sun. Roots dig into soil. All wait hungrily to be given.

The deep urge in our souls wants grounding, needs light, longs for living water, too. We cannot grow on our own any more than any plant in nature can. At the core we know that of our own selves we can do nothing. We are only what we are given, what we are able to receive and return. Fundamentally we are beggars. Every living thing in this world is a beggar.

Summer is a fullness born of need. How wonderfully strange and freeing it is to accept this basic poverty. It makes for mutual acceptance of a fundamental emptiness. It makes us understand that we are part of the whole and therefore one with it. Isn't our task then to wait in dignity upon what brings us life and so to wait upon each other?

In lush abundance how relieving it is to be stripped down to essentials, to the bare truth that we are small, insignificant, and precious. This is what is real. To this essential poverty all is given.

The Tasks at Hand

In a twinkling I can go from smelling the sweet air, loving the morning, relishing time outdoors to just plain getting through whatever the task is that I have at hand. What happens?

I've turned myself into a function. I've lost my person. Everything around me becomes an object to manipulate or an obstacle to overcome. What makes me human—the capacity to relate, to meet and be met—disappears. I've become responsible instead of response-able.

Must it be so to get done the things we have to do? I don't think we want to believe that. But the truth is that we slip. So often I find myself turning into a garden robot with the start button on—dig, weed, prune, till, snip. I turn snippy. I crash. I have allowed tasks to overwhelm me. I've lost all sense of leisure. When we let our survival mind take over we lose both what centers all work and what makes it sacred.

"Take your time," we say. We mean, "Give yourself time." We mean, respect your personhood. We mean, be present to what is in the moment. If I am left out of my own heart, who is slashing at the bushes? In such a state can I be trusted? I don't think so.

We long to be saved within time, to feel that Holy Presence that allows us to perceive what is at hand and to be present enough to recognize it as gift.

God dwells outside of time,
outside of what you call "past"
and "future."

God is now
where your soul, too, belongs.

Companion Planting

The companions we keep are important. We have friends and acquaintances that strengthen us, that help us to be more of who we really are. And there are others by whom we are crowded or drained and, yes, outright threatened.

In the garden this is also true. Pole beans like carrots. Lettuce gets along with the radish. Basil, tomatoes, and peppers thrive with one another. I like to plant my garden this way when I can.

As I put the oriental chives of the onion family with the roses, I wonder, why not put friends together? Is that not loving? Why extend further? Why risk failure? "Love your enemies," I hear my mind reminding me. "Greater love has no one than to give their life for a friend." It doesn't say enemy!

It seems important to sort this. When a person hurts us or someone we love, what are the limits of love? When one plant overwhelms another and chokes its life, shouldn't we intervene? Don't both plants have a right to their lives? Could love be meant here as spaciousness, as recognition—that our enemy has as much right to exist as we do? Are we able to hold that understanding without going into conflict, and without surrendering our own right to be? Perhaps love here is compassion for all that we are unable to love? So many thoughts are planted side by side. Where are the answers to the unanswerable?

Reasoning never makes a thing
absolutely true.

Faced with challenge,
what you are in that moment is revealed.

The strangest things crop up together.
Look at jewelweed,
how peacefully it grows with poison ivy.

Answers come in the living of them.

Cultivating

The romaine and the oak leaf lettuce is up, arugula and spinach. I see signs of early peas. It's all new, tender growth. The garden is waking up as when my heart opens with new inspiration, sudden hope, and unexpected joy. I feel the tender promise of greening. But now I also notice how I want to hurry things along, help the growing to grow. I know this is lethal. But to me, in this enthusiasm, common sense has no sense. How often we want to be sure of what is already true—how strange a human heart can be! Even with evidence that things are as they should be, we can be grasping for more certainty.

I feel how eager I am to go. There seems to be no stopping me. So I fetch the garden tools from under the bulkhead. Could I just pause long enough to hear, "First, do no harm"? What if all of us could pause to hear those words?

Fork in hand, I sit on the ground at plant level. This equalizes things a bit. Now I can see what has taken place over time. It seems hard to believe that from the small seeds I placed here only three weeks ago so much has grown.

"Make haste slowly. Be light." I hear the warning. Could it be that even as the soil of life is lifted and turned, we may feel we are being turned and lifted as well? Could discernment guide us to consider the whole picture before we dive in with even happy hopes of helping? Might this be what it means to be cultivated?

Be in awe of all that is alive.

Be in natural wonder.

It is the pace of peace.

Staking

When the peonies emerge they are rusty red, blood colored. We, too, are born in the color of blood. The stalks thrust up in a row, claim a welcome and the birthright to be allowed to grow into full stature. By early summer the buds are set on long, elegant stems.

In the back by the fence they stand proudly, ready to burst into blossom. But I know once the buds open, the flower heads will bend low to the ground. The sheer weight of them always surprises me.

When anything blooms it is a weighty matter, a matter to celebrate, an occasion to be glad. How fine to birth a child, graduate from school, get a promotion, retire, or do any of our human blossoming!

We forget though, there is weight to it, and like peonies we need staking for the fruiting effort and also for the time when the harsh winds come, the rain, the bad times in life. That support may perhaps be most essential when we are full out in the open fragrance of our blooming. In success we are very vulnerable, easily exploited, prone to be caught up in ourselves. We need the sturdy stake and the garden twine of friends and family to keep us steady. We need to rely on a sense of God's presence, stabilized by the source of all fruition.

See how the ants in the peonies
are loving every blossom.

They burrow in to praise,
and are not worried in delight.

Be glad in the moment of blooming.
Without bidding
the morrow will come.

Weeding

On my knees in the herb garden, I am surrounded by weeds, by too much growth, by crowding and seeming chaos. Could I turn this weeding into prayer?

Today, after longed-for rain, the earth smells damp and good. I want to feel the earth of my being, too. As I pull up the chickweed, the clover, the dandelions, and the plantain, my compost bucket fills with what I have no use for. A strange satisfaction overtakes me. So immediate is the pleasure of making space. I love the openness between the basil and the thyme. Plain, brown earth has a beauty all its own.

The morning passes. The bucket fills. Silent and sustaining, the earth is more and more visible between the plants. This weeding lets me know what is happening here in the herb bed, what is happening in my life. Now it's clearer what needs thinning, feeding, replacing, or ignoring.

I can see this act of clearing will let established plants fill out and flourish. So, too, when we clear our schedule, our unnecessary business, our lack of focus, we will see our true commitments. Then, like established plants, they have a chance to flourish and grow. As we weed our lives we grow freer. More and more, room for nothing beckons us to heartfelt ground.

A weeded garden is a restful sight.

But, unweeded, it can be dynamic.
See how plants fight
for their patch in the sun.

The strong ones survive
and not always the handsome.
Perhaps they *are the essential plants*
no one has found
the right use for as yet.

Can you trust that
out of chaos comes the new?
Order and beauty have fooled many.

Blooming

The roses are glorious, opening, opening, opening. Their fragrance is delicate and penetrating. Flowers have often been used to symbolize the heart, the receptive soul. We can see this in old cathedrals where color and light shine through their rose windows to remind us of the soul's capacity for openness, for vulnerability.

We are often afraid of full blooming, of holding nothing back. And how much we also want it. Is not the place we can be hurt, and the place we are fulfilled, the very same place?

I touch the soft satin of the rose petals. Here is pink gold. Here is unfolding, unfolding until the petals give way and float to the ground, the free fall of fulfillment. This morning I watch the wind lift one petal, gently loosening it. The petal drifts down to my feet, offering its silent wisdom—blossom unafraid and let go.

Your rose petals are turning brown
in the compost along with onion skins,
eggshells, and carrot scrapings.

How universal is rot,
how inclusive.
Its aroma is a rich mix
of that which was
and that which is not yet.

It is the scent of possibility,
laced with the nectar of roses.

Edging

The edger is a steel half-moon I push into thick grass that has wandered into the lower border. A clod of earth is pried loose. Roots dangle, white and exposed. I shake off the soil and push the edger in again. Such slow going creates a line between the border and the lawn. When the line is tidy and deep, the grass stays where it belongs and the border is defined with clean and beautiful clarity.

How often boundaries are fussy or neglected between people, the communication edge somehow not there—clarifying expectations, illuminating misconceptions, defining duties, saying "yes" or "no" clearly. This is easy to see here in the garden. I don't mind running roughshod on the grass. It can take it where a person might not.

What if we could really trust ourselves and others to make a true line where it is needed for our good and theirs? Could we use an edger on ourselves as well, to keep out of interactions that are not ours to be in? It's hard work to be so conscious—clod by clod to see the exposed roots of sloppy thinking, of unexamined motives.

I shake the soil loose from the divot in my hand. Exposure is not comfortable. "Look at the boundaries," I tell myself. "What is God's will here?" What if we could just stop long enough to ask that question and sense into the answer? Could we bear knowing that what we sense may be wrong and then live with the doubt?

Even now
every living thing is surrounded
by God's awareness.

Your intentions are already known,
as well as the efforts you make
to be faithful to them.

Stand on the sharp yet unknowing
edge and bear down.
The final results are not up to you.

Bittersweet

Deadly nightshade, stinging nettle, poison ivy, bittersweet. They are rampant, profuse and clever in camouflage. Tucked under other plants they wind through bushes and trees affirming, it seems, their right to be part of, if not to dominate the garden.

As much as I pull them out, they are back every year, ready to participate, to climb up healthy plants and choke them, for that matter. Why should they not have their bit of sun, their piece of heaven? Even now at the top of the evergreens the bittersweet reaches into air with a languid tendril, searching for further purchase.

Their persistence is staggering. Their insistence is awesome. Could we be as robust in pursuit of our connections, spiritual or otherwise, as they are of their growth?

The names of these plants are ominous—stinging, bitter, poisonous, deadly. From one perspective their names are true of some of the qualities of their growth habits. They grow on other plants, dominate and kill what sustains them. Are we humans not doing this to the earth?

I give these vines due respect, and I also pull them. They will be back as will the deadly, the poisonous, the bitter, the stinging parts of myself. They are the tendencies that live in my inner garden as much as they live in the backyard. I must admit of them. I must watch them.

In time,
everything adjusts
and comes to new balance.

When the host is exhausted,
the parasite dies.
The laws of nature are just
and inexorable.
They are fundamentally kind.

Fertilizing

Out among the vegetable beds the big bag of fertilizer stands open. I dip the scooper in. The smell of fish and chemicals is strong.

Everything needs feeding to grow. I sprinkle the beds with a fine dusting. I fork up the soil, mound the earth for a second planting. The soil is light with air. Everything is ready and full of possibility.

These beds are like dreams that need nurture. We are like them—God's dreams. We need to be fed to come true.

Feeding too much
burns the soil.
Seeds do not germinate.
The life in them is stunned.

In feeding anything, take care
that innate potential is not stolen.

When too much fertilizer takes
the life from a seed,
whose dream is being lived?

Dry days and nights
are the times when God removes
too much feeding.

Trust this deeper love,
this freeing love.

Japanese Beetles

Here they are again in their iridescent lacquer. They appear just when the beans begin to grow and the Peace rose opens a second time.

Deep in rose nectar they copulate and revel, consuming, consuming, consuming. By afternoon the roses are half eaten, the petals brown, my careful planting desiccated. One by one I pick them up in their satiated stupor, pop them into a Mason jar and close the lid. All these weeks of work are erased in a moment. So quick is destruction, me of them, they of the roses and the sweet bean leaves.

The jar in my hand is full of movement, of milling, of crawling and failed attempts to fly. Soon the beetles will be corpses, the green light of their wings snuffed out.

"How can I do this?" I ask myself. God's gift of life is equal. This is a beetle's world as well as mine. Even so I screw the lid down further on the jar.

Asking questions is easy.
Taking responsibility is another thing.

What will you do tomorrow?

Midsummer Cleanup

By now the pansies are leggy with dead transparent flowers, like old moth wings hanging over the edges of the planter. By July the peony blossoms are on the ground as if a shredder had mowed through them. Red poppy petals sigh away in the breeze. Their fine ruffled taffeta melts in the sun. Only the black seed heads stand alone on their stalks—a constellation of black stars.

In August the marigolds begin to shrivel. Their little brown purses are drawn together tightly. I am out in the heat of the garden, removing old blooms. How fleeting is summer's flowering season!

With a soft thud the brown dahlia heads plop into my garden pail. There is a basic sadness when good things are over. I want this task to be simple and true. Here on the way to the compost is the detritus of blossoming. It's another kind of beauty. I am grateful to have witnessed the time of blooming and to also witness the decline—my own decline as well.

Can we see life in a pail full of dead flowers, the rhythm of blossoming and dying, the infinite cycle of emerging and disappearing, of acceptance and surrender and return? Can we let what once was all promise go to decay and future soil? Can we learn not to look backwards, not to regret, and not to anticipate decline before it is here?

Your feet are not lost.
You are standing on the ground.

Earth supports you in life,
and you are held by it in death.

The elements of earth
are your very substance.
Where is the decline?

Watering

In the heat of late summer and early fall the garden needs so much water. In the heat of a life the inner thirst grows. The more we put out, the more we need to be filled with living water. On our own we can do very little, and that not for long. There is always this fundamental necessity to be infused with God's love and energizing power.

I unroll the hose. There are the familiar kinks, which show up time and time again as do the kinks in my capacity to give my full attention. The green rubber folds over, a stubborn habit. No water will come through. In my mind, too, an interrupting thought lies across my attention. I have a kink as solid and full of habit as the ones in the hose.

Slowly I pull out the full length of the hose and lay it where it needs to be before I turn on the water. Inside, too, I must unroll my full attention. Old habits of thought twist themselves into kinks and knots. We will be forced to acknowledge this again and again.

Now in the evening light the water begins to flow. I adjust the nozzle and stand where I need to for the water to reach each part of the garden. In prayer, too, we stand and wait. Both inside and outside have need of a thorough soaking. The rushing sound of the water feels comforting. The steady stream turns gold and shimmers as it catches the last rays of the sun. The garden waits for this water. Our lives wait for Presence to pour in.

Thirst is a good prayer.

Be true to your longing.

Autumn

Autumn

The plants in the garden are giving their all. Stems and leaves surrender their energy to fruiting. The days are shorter, the air cooler. Autumn is a ripeness, an urgency to complete, to go to fruit and seed, to give to the future. Our lives, too, must be allowed to mature, to be able to give to others. We do not bear fruit for ourselves. We bear fruit for life itself.

It is a strange paradox that fulfillment is so much about surrender. We recognize ourselves best when we give our selves fully. It is how we discover what we essentially are, or rather what we have been allowed to become from the gifts that were given us.

Now the leaves are turning tawny or burning red and bright with gold. The joy of completion blazes in every direction. Fulfillment demands that we let go. We must fall into unknowing again, open to an expectation without intention. Then nonattachment can be felt as the greatest fruit, that divine freedom that lets life live us.

Witnessing

I prune, cultivate, weed, water, harvest. My efforts influence what happens, but what about how the garden influences me? The few hours I work are nothing in comparison to the hours the garden burgeons and fruits. It does it all on its own. In my life, too, so much happens that I have no apparent effort in creating.

What a slow process it is to learn that an essential part of working, in a garden or in life, is to let what is happening happen! Of course, we must do our part, but equally we must allow ourselves and our circumstances to simply be, to evolve without force.

The garden holds an invisible power we are invited to witness. How amazing to sense oneself rooted in a dynamic and holy leisure, an organic confidence that we are held and sustained by the ground of being. Then even dark, dead, and barren parts of ourselves have an authentic place to be. Centered in the deep conviction that what needs to happen is occurring, we learn to let go, to trust infinite timing, not our own.

For a change, do nothing.
Do it fully without fear.

See how in doing nothing,
everything is somehow done.

Harvesting

The second planting of pole beans is ready to be picked. The beans hang long and sweet in clusters on the vine. Like lanterns, the tomatoes glow red. Right under my eyes the zucchini is growing another inch. Deep purple eggplants are heavy and plump. The vegetable garden is full, full, full.

How to appreciate this bounty? I can't always take it in. Having so much produce I sometimes feel burdened. The garden becomes a blur of muchness, and in my mind I turn it into a command to consume.

If I froze the vegetables or canned them I would follow the age-old rural pattern of storing for winter. But I don't. I simply feast, share, and, yes, waste. Too much can erase gratitude, as much as too little can. How many times have we not seen, from sheer overwhelm, how a child cries when given too many birthday gifts? In such circumstances she can't play with any of them.

I would like so much for the measure of my gratitude to be as ample as the fruitfulness of the garden. "To them that have much shall be given." This can be true only if we receive, if we are empty enough to take nothing for granted.

Whether witnessed,
received, used, or wasted,
the joy of fruiting
hums even in the tiniest autumn berry.

Join the joy!
You are invited.

Pruning

In spring the roses are pruned the first time to free them of winterkill. They are cut back to green wood. In the autumn, the roses are pruned a second time—cut to be able to bear the harshness of winter.

As I snip with the pruning shears and cut with the Skil saw I wonder, what is growing at cross purposes with the central thrust of my life? What enthusiasm has me risking a detour from my deepest intention?

Standing back I am able to notice the shape of a plant or a bush. Standing back and looking at our lives we can discern what to cut—the whole branch, the small twig, and all that must be nipped in the bud. I stake a small tree with guy wires to strengthen its upright tendency. Any time we stand back we can see where we might need more emotional support. I train the clematis up the back fence. Standing back we can see where we must train ourselves in new ways, refraining from a bad habit or starting a healthful one.

This is time-consuming! We must learn to take small, frequent steps back to see the corrections to be made. Then with small steps forward we can cut the unnecessary, the even now so yearningly appealing. We know that winterkill will come, the life kill, the unexpected. It is good to prune, to cut back to essentials, to where life really is, where it can be sustained when the cold comes. It is painstaking and so very slow.

It won't be long
before a storm will prune
what is ready to let go.
It will be clean and swift.

Be your own storm.

Seed Keeping

The impatiens have set their seed pods—fat, green, little purses. With the slightest touch the pods explode in my waiting hands. There must be ten to twenty tiny seeds in each powerful package. Here is new life ready to root and develop, given a new season, given a chance.

Holding these fine white seeds I feel God's nearness, the sheer profusion of God's gifting. All around me is given-ness. Within me is given-ness. Just a small word, some ordinary event, or a simple touch can burst the seed-pod of the self. Instantly there are new possibilities. We must open to let the hidden splendor out.

Carefully, I place the impatiens seeds in envelopes for keeping—salmon, white, pink. They will be ready for spring. Can we allow the seeds of new life to be stored in our hearts? Can we be confident there will be spring? Can we really trust that what can sprout, will? It has to—because the sheer law of God's joy commands it.

The inherent exuberance of nature
is to spill and squander.

In spring,
does the maple hoard its seeds?
It keeps nothing.
At its fruiting,
the ground is carpeted with wings.

That which has fallen will rise.
Green canopies will cover you yet
with generous shade.

Raking

The Japanese maple catches the morning sun. There is a vibrant red, a slow brilliance developing over weeks. The tree is on fire. Then one day almost all the leaves fall. The ground becomes a red carpet. I like having the carpet there. I like to scuff my feet through the dry, shriveling leaves. To be lighthearted with what is over and done with is a great gift.

In winter's early rains the leaves mat down, killing grass in the same way I may keep sorrow too close, too long, until it kills my joy. I need to rake now! We all need to bring to the surface pains, regrets, grief, old angers that still lie around in the front lawns of our lives.

I hear the raspy sound of the rake's tines as they scratch the ground. I think of what is painful in my life. There's a decision here, a decision to notice, acknowledge, gather, and deliberately remove. I cart the maple leaves in the blue plastic tarp to the compost pile in the back. I need to turn them over to the deep processes of nature. Inside I need to turn what is done and gone over to my God.

Even after I rake, some leaves are left. I see them rolling over the lawn in the wind. Like small sorrows, and lingering pain, even they will be gone. The habit of regret must be allowed to turn to soil. We need less to be reformed and cleaned up than to align with the deep composting of God's love.

Raking things up,
raking things over—
it is possible to have too much conscience.

"Be still and know,"
you have been told.
It is God
that is God.

Cleaning Up

"She cleaned up on that one," we say when winning a game or making a good deal of some kind. It's autumn now. When I put the garden to bed I feel the gift it has been. Indeed, I've cleaned up.

Yes, the fallen sticks, the brown stems of the black-eyed Susans, the wilted leaves of the daylilies are the remains of a season. But as I gather them up I remember the blossoms, the vibrant green leaves, the branching new growth. There is a truthful beauty in these stalks—upright and weathered. Brown, hollow, and dry they tell of life lived to the full. They are icons of surrender.

My own life is in Autumn now. I want to live the beauty of these years. Cleaning up, I know we are not what we have or what we have done. We are what we have been given. It is the gift of this season in life to be as simple as a brown stalk in falling light—that spiritually bare, that naked.

The young, the old,
the rotten, the fertile,
the ugly, the beautiful,
the poisonous, the sublime,
the forgotten, the remembered—
all belong in the infinite mix.
Are they not part of soil?

There is nothing that is without use—
nothing left out of the whole.
You are there, part of the Holy.

Lying Fallow

The gardening season has come to a close. I walk around the yard. The wind is cold, the sky gray. I stand by the vegetable beds. They lie fallow now, flat and open. A few weeds are left in them. Looking forlorn, a volunteer arugula is growing in a corner despite the cold.

The beds seem barren. But I know lying fallow is different from doing nothing. All the doing or ceasing of doing—which is a kind of doing as well—is not the issue. In the interior life lying fallow has a dynamic nakedness to it. It is an abject state before God in which we are open to being used or abandoned, loved or ignored. It is a radical placement of trust that, destroyed or raised up, we will remain open to the mystery that made us.

Even under the richest growth and abundance, is there not a deep fallowness at work that we often ignore? We are very afraid of it. Perhaps that pure quality of humble, willing "there-ness" is the closest state in which we can sense God. It requires emptiness. It requires everything.

To lie fallow is a gift. We don't really know how to do it. Rather we are done by it or undone by it. The moments we are allowed to be in that condition are times of gratitude. It is from there that our freedom comes. It is where authentic being exists. Any fruitfulness arises from that surrendered openness. It is there that God makes each of us a fertile ground, a bearing soil.

Be willing,
imitate the vast permission
that is God's love.

Be fallow,
turned
into fertile ground.

Four Seasons

Four Seasons

A whole year in the garden, a whole year in my life, working the soil. I labor with my small self, struggle with all its engagements, opinions, and doings. Insights arise when I dig and weed in my life. They may be small and only relevant to me. That is the chance I take, a chance we all must take. It matters that we take it, for we are more alike than we are different. We have basic needs for food and shelter. We also have a profound need for meaning. Is it not our basic work as persons to make of our lives a garden of meaning, a garden whose fruits we can share?

We do not do this alone. All along, the soil is there, perennial and quiet. It is mute unless we consciously lean our ears towards it and try to hear. It is from the earth itself that we have evolved. We are made of it and express it. The words humus, human, and humility are deeply connected. We are soil. Our beings express the earth and contribute to it. Now, unless we listen deeply, we may destroy what sustains us. It is crucial that we feel that deep, intrinsic connection.

Any time we make a garden, even a tiny one, we are in the work of remembering. Working the soil, cultivating our inner ground, we have a chance to appreciate and praise the great gift of life and the earth that sustains us. We are held by something so beyond our ken and so essentially unknowable. We call it God though no word can name it. Humming through us, through the ground, through all things, it asks us to be particular, to be living expressions, to be sons and daughters of earth and to care for life itself. It asks us to be fruitful—to tend the garden, to protect the garden, to share the garden, to be the garden.

One who plants a garden,

plants happiness.

CHINESE PROVERB